Broken To Win

Broken To Win

Change The Trajectory of Your Life!

Lester M. Cox

Foreword by Dr. Donald R. Hudson

XULON PRESS

Xulon Press
2301 Lucien Way #415
Maitland, FL 32751
407.339.4217
www.xulonpress.com

© 2022 by LESTER M. COX

All rights reserved solely by the author. The author guarantees all contents are original and do not infringe upon the legal rights of any other person or work. No part of this book may be reproduced in any form without the permission of the author.

Due to the changing nature of the Internet, if there are any web addresses, links, or URLs included in this manuscript, these may have been altered and may no longer be accessible. The views and opinions shared in this book belong solely to the author and do not necessarily reflect those of the publisher. The publisher therefore disclaims responsibility for the views or opinions expressed within the work.

Unless otherwise indicated, Scripture quotations taken from the King James Version (KJV)–*public domain*. Scripture quotations taken from the English Standard Version (ESV). Copyright © 2001 by Crossway, a publishing ministry of Good News Publishers. Used by permission. All rights reserved.

Paperback ISBN-13: 978-1-66285-537-5
Ebook ISBN-13: 978-1-66285-538-2

In loving memory of:

My parents, Rev. Carlos and Minister Corrine Cox, who have given me a Godly heritage that keeps me in the good and the bad times.

My mentor, Bishop Goodwin Campbell Smith (Bermuda) a man of great wisdom, insight, and integrity.

*Bishop Teuton Stubbs (Bahamas), you always reminded me that I must **"stoop to conquer,"** and to not let the prophetic words of success spoken over my life fall to the ground.*

Broken To Win – The Foreword

Brokenness is hard to swallow because it leaves us with a bitter taste. It is a real part of life that we cannot avoid, no matter how hard we try to do so. It is a real part of life that we seldom want to face, entertain, or admit exists because it takes a heavy toll on our life in every aspect. Brokenness is a part of life that we attempt to hide at times because we prefer to always appear whole and strong in the sight of others, particularly if we declare that we have faith in God.

However, one of the common denominators of the human existence is brokenness. No matter what our beginnings has been, or where we are presently in our life journey, or what our future may be, we are all subject to "broken moments" and "broken experiences."

If we are honest, we can confess that we are familiar with brokenness and how it feels, while wondering if anything good would come out of such experiences. I have discovered in my own journey of brokenness that there exists underneath our fragments the possibilities of winning that is not always obvious. Sometimes the pain and disappointments of our brokenness blinds us from seeing that we can still win.

Brokenness is part of the human equation and is unavoidable. No matter what our spiritual aptitude is, or how deep our faith in God is, or what our station and position in life is, experiencing brokenness from time to time is absolute. No one is exempt from this reality. Whether our brokenness is by our own making, or by God's will, or by His permissive will, or perhaps by a natural occurrence, each of us has an appointment with brokenness, and we must make the appointment whether we want to or not.

The reality of brokenness can be earth shaking and faith testing. It can cause us to question ourselves and question the positive possibilities of life, as well as question God. We must have an understanding that there is an alternative reality that is beyond our brokenness, and that alternative reality is that our brokenness does not have to be the concluding chapter of our life story, and those broken moments and experiences can help us win even when we are feeling as if we are losing. Sometimes brokenness is what we need to get us in a position where we can begin living like winners.

In this book, *Broken To Win*, the author, Lester Cox, reminds us from his own experiences that brokenness can lead to winning. He speaks volumes of truth and fresh discoveries in a place that few people dare to venture, and that place is where life seems to fall to pieces, even while being faithful to the Creator, and while we are attempting to do our best to live our best life possible.

In this literary masterpiece the author addresses brokenness from a positive, empowering, and life-changing perspective, without losing sight of reality. He keeps it real.

There are books on the market that deal with subjects such as brokenness and overcoming it, but from a theoretical perspective versus from real life episodes. However, interwoven in the pages of this literary masterpiece, this author deals with brokenness, and becoming a winner in spite of it, from the depths of his heart, soul and experiences with God, who is the mender of our broken pieces. Lester Cox addresses brokenness and winning from his life experiences, as well as his experiences with God, through faith and not from theory.

This book deals with winning despite our brokenness from a Christian and faith perspective. However, even though it is composed from a Christian and faith perspective, it connects to each of us regardless of our religion, faith orientation, race, or social class. It deals with a real aspect of life with which we are all familiar or will become familiar.

The author challenges us to face our brokenness, which can be painful. However, he does not leave us hanging there. Instead, he shows us how to overcome our brokenness and begin being winners. He shows us how to pick up the pieces in our broken journey and move into a winner's circle.

In these prolific pages, Lester Cox provides the reader with a map that leads to fresh discoveries, no matter how broken we are; He shows us how to discover more about ourselves as we encounter episodes of brokenness. He also shows us how to discover more about God as we enter His divine presence, as He unfolds His unique plan for us to win despite how broken we may be. Lester Cox offers us a way to experience our despair turning into hope, our sadness transformed into joy, and our lives becoming whole, despite how disjointed our lives may be in the present. Welcome to **BROKEN TO WIN**! It is your time to win!

Dr. Donald R. Hudson
Motivation 4 Impact Ministries
Dallas, Texas

U.S.A.

Acknowledgements

Habakkuk 2:2-3 (KJV) declares, *"And the LORD answered me, and said, "Write the vision, and make it plain upon tables, that he may run that readeth it. For the vision is yet for an appointed time, but at the end it shall speak, and not lie: though it tarry, wait for it; because it will surely come, it will not tarry."* This scripture reveals with great clarity that a vision CANNOT be accomplished by one single person. While one may think and then record it, there are others who will take it and run to perform it. With that being said, I could not go any further into this book without first acknowledging the gifts that God has placed into my life to run this vision into completion.

First and foremost, I give thanks to my God, Jehovah. He is my Lord and Savior, the Restorer of my soul, and the Giver of my peace. In the midst of my brokenness, I have asked **Psalms 51:11 -** *"Cast me not away from thy presence; and take not thy Holy Spirit from me."* On so many occasions You've granted my plea, and for that, I humbly say thank you. When I look at this work that You have completed, this message of being broken to win, I now understand all that I have had to face. Thank you for entrusting me with this assignment and for staying beside me along the way. I'm forever grateful to You.

To my editor, Ms. Alexis Gardiner (Nassau, Bahamas), a woman of excellence and of kindred spirit; a woman of great faith, who without fear has prophetically declared this book as **"God's Next Bestseller"**, I graciously say thank you! Thank you for your commitment and diligence in ensuring that I dotted my I's and crossed my T's, thereby producing this work of excellence. I thank God for this divine connection and am eternally grateful that you are on my team. I look forward to many more books together!

To my publisher, Xulon Press (Salem Media Group), and my initial contact in the person of Jeff Fitzgerald, Thank you for your guidance in bringing this work to publication. Thank you for the many telephone conversations and emails and for always being a listening ear. Thanks to you and your hardworking team, my ideas have now become reality, and you have exceeded my every expectation. God bless you!

To Apostle Valentino Williams, Senior Pastor of Life Changers Ministries International (Nassau, Bahamas) – what can I truly say? From the conversations to the prayers and so much more, you have blessed my life tremendously. Thank you for all the people to whom you have introduced me to. You are a friend and brother indeed, and I appreciate and love you and your family to life!

To my sister-in-law, Ms. Jackie Lacey Seymour (Lake Mary, Florida by way of Bermuda), we did it! When you released the words you had for me, the simple instruction - **"Write the book,"** you couldn't have had better timing. I took those words to heart because they were the confirmation that I needed to continue this great work. Without even knowing it, you catapulted me into completion. For your obedience and your willingness to share, I say thank you. Now I can say it is done!

Acknowledgements

Finally, I extend sincere thanks to my Bishop and spiritual covering, Bishop Vaughn and Lady Narlene McGlaughlin, Covenant Fellowship International and The Potters House International Ministries (Jacksonville, Florida). You have sheltered my family and me when we were going through our 'wilderness experience'. Thank you for all your love, support, words of encouragement, and for the tangible sacrifices that you've both made for me and my family. Thank you for looking out for our children while they were attending university and for helps too numerous to mention! I love you beyond words, and I trust that God will give me the means and the longevity to bless you both beyond measure.

Table of Contents

Dedication..xvii

Preface   xix

PART ONE: SHATTERED

Chapter One: The Impact 3

Chapter Two: The Aftermath 9

PART TWO: BROKEN FRAGMENTS

Chapter Three: Facing Truth........................... 19

Chapter Four: A Purpose 29

Chapter Five: Jagged Edges 41

PART THREE: THE ASSEMBLING

Chapter Six: Fragility.....................................51

Chapter Seven: Piece by Piece.......................... 57

Chapter Eight: Wholeness 65

Conclusion – To the Winners 69

Dedication

This book is dedicated to my beautiful wife Vanessa, without whom I would not have been able to make it through the many challenges that we have faced together in our lives. Thank you for your support and encouragement along the way. Thank you for your wisdom and strength, for unselfishly sharing with me the gift of faith that God has so graciously given to you. I love you more than words would allow me to say.

To our beautiful children, Lester Matthew and Hilary Amanda, you have brought so much laughter and stability to our lives. You have been Godly treasures wrapped in earthen vessels, and we thank God for you. I know it is tough at times being the Bishop's children, but you have both made me so proud. You have given me such a sense of purpose in life and have taught me how to be a family even in the most trying of times. Always remember that I love and cherish you both.

To First Lady Ruby Smith, the lovely wife of the late Bishop Goodwin Campbell Smith, I thank you on behalf of my family and myself for the abundance of support that you have shown us. May God richly bless you!

To my family, too large to list by name, thank you for remaining "family". Through the laughter, the tears, the heartache and the pain; through the joys and sorrows, the frustrations and heated discussions; through the hard times and the easy times, you have remained that constant support and backing that I needed. I appreciate each and every one of you, and I love you dearly.

To families everywhere who are trying to hold the pieces of life together, even in the toughest of times, in particular those at Word of Truth Ministries International (Bahamas), a people on a collision course filled with destiny and greatness I declare healing in your broken pieces. I have found great pleasure in being your Bishop, and I commend you for your strength and tenacity. I encourage you in Christ to continue to press towards the mark for the prize of the high calling of God in Christ Jesus **(Philippians 3:14, KJV)**.

Last but not least, to all the survivors who are reading this book, I encourage you to remain strong. Remember that it is in Christ that you are winners. For this battle is already won, and you are victorious!

Preface

Brokenness is an unavoidable 'rite of passage' that everyone has to face at some point or the other in their lives. It's the part of life that no one looks forward to and the part of life that people seldom talk about.

Webster's dictionary defines brokenness as violently separated into parts; shattered, damaged, altered by breaking; or disrupted by change. But, before we go any further, I want you to ponder for a moment on these questions. What should we do when we feel broken and battered? Who should we turn to when it seems as though everything inside of us and around us is crumbling? How should we cope with the pressures that at times appear to be so insurmountable? How can we distinguish the voice of truth from that which is false?

To get the best answers to these questions I must first refer you to Jehovah God. He is my foundation and a proven friend, lawyer, and counsellor to those who need it. He has been strength, peace, and a way maker for me during the times when I thought there was none. He is my everything and I have full confidence in ALL of who He is. As a matter of fact, I can say undoubtedly that once you get to know God, the answers to those probing questions become easier to find. You see, the answer **IS** Him!

Jehovah God has the answer for every question that man can think or ask. He is our one TRUE solution. Only He can make silent the noise of the world that surrounds us. Only He can bring peace to one's heart and mind while in the midst of chaos, frustration, and brokenness. The key to attaining this peace, however, is **BEING STILL**. Stillness allows you to bring intentional focus to God's voice and all that He wants to say to you. It is there, in His words, that true peace is found.

Brokenness is not by any stretch of the imagination an easy period to face. As a matter of fact, it's life-altering! Along with the pressure to simply endure it, brokenness brings a host of thoughts and feelings that can test your strength, your faith, and ultimately anything foundational that you've built your life upon. It even has the ability to bring you face to face with whether you TRULY know God; and depending on the state that you are in, you can find yourself wondering anything from whether God is really real to whether He is truly able to deliver you out of your situation.

Fueled by the doubt, condemnation, and low self-worth brought about by brokenness, a person's views and perception of themselves and their situation can also be distorted. For example, some people begin to view their life condition as a punishment, while others grow to accept the way things are as their fate. Such misconceptions only enhance the state of brokenness that these people are in, ultimately making reclamation a bit harder to see or believe.

When challenged by brokenness, even pride and selfishness disappear. The succession of events that occur during this time can strip you of all your dignity and cause your spirit to become weary, which further results in feelings of impatience, discontentment and mental fatigue. You begin to feel like throwing in the towel and can even find yourself thinking - *'What's the point of living,'* but this is where you must draw the line.

God's ultimate desire is that we trust Him in all things, and this is why tests of brokenness come. Without these tests, our faith wouldn't be perfected. Thankfully, we do not enter these periods alone. Amidst all the noise that brokenness brings to our lives, there is yet still a quiet voice speaking – God's Holy Spirit, and if you listen close enough, you will hear Him speaking words of hope to your heart and mind. This is because He knows that the expectation of things getting better will cause you to endure. In other words, this hope will strengthen your faith, and strong faith produces endurance!

When we were enlisted into humanity by being born, we had no idea where life would take us and what experiences we would encounter. We weren't made privy to the demands of life and what we would need to survive. In fact, only God knew. He knew what we would face, how far we would go, and who we would become. His Word (the Bible) was left as a manuscript and game plan equipped with guidelines and faith-building reminders to help us navigate through various life situations. One popular yet powerful faith-builder is found in **Jeremiah 29:11-13, (KJV)** *"For I know the thoughts that I think towards you, saith the Lord, thoughts of peace, and not of evil, to give you an expected end. Then shall ye call upon me, and ye shall go and pray unto me, and I will hearken unto you. And ye shall seek me, and find me, when ye shall search for me with all your heart."* What a great reminder to have when faced with the impenitent issues of life!

Romans 11:33 states that God's ways are pass finding out, indicating that His methods of refining us can be hard to understand at times. But total reliance on God and His infinite power while in the midst of brokenness will only help you to develop strength and *stickability* as a believer. When God sees that you are willing to stick with Him, even with your back against the wall, He will be further compelled to move on your behalf, and in ways that will exceed your every expectation.

Broken To Win has been written and purposed to take you from a place of brokenness to one of wholeness. Through the use of my testimony and God's divine inspiration and impartation, you will come face to face with the realization that brokenness does not have to be a permanent state for you. You will be reminded that life is all about the choices that you make, and you will see the power that lies in your choice to have faith and stand strong even while in the midst of turbulence.

This book is a map of discovery, discovery not only of you, but of God and His plans to see you through to success. It's a much-needed journey of honesty and reflection that will bring you face to face with your true self. You see, oftentimes than not, when we think or talk about the failures and misfortunes of our lives, we fail to acknowledge the role we play in the outcome. We even fail to see our contribution to the situation and how God wants to bring us out. But after reading this book, you will come to understand how your posture, your mindset, and your choices help to position you for deliverance. You will also be empowered to take control of your destiny by firstly adjusting your mindset, and then by remitting total and complete trust to God.

The songwriter said, *"It won't always be like this,"* and that is the message that **Broken To Win** has come to deliver. Your despair will be changed to hope, your sadness to joy, and your brokenness to wholeness. I believe that after reading this book your way of thinking and seeing will change. Your posture will be adjusted, and the way that you deal with circumstances will be modified. You will begin to see that through true surrender and reliance on Jehovah God, your season of unrelenting losses and failures can be changed to countless victories. There is a refreshing and renewing on its way to you. Open your spirit to God and allow your road to victory to begin...right here and right now!

With all that has been said, *"I declare wholeness into your spirit as you read this book. May your life be changed for the better! May you allow God to work His plan out in you to the very end! May you know that, despite where you are right now, you are victorious, you are an overcomer, and you have been BROKEN TO WIN!"*

Blessings,
Bishop Lester M. Cox

Part One
SHATTERED

CHAPTER ONE
The Impact

Imagine for a moment a precious vase sitting high on a shelf, an expensive china glass placed on a counter, a bottle lying on the side of the road – empty, not seeming to bother anyone. No matter how expensive or how cheap these items may appear to be, they all have one thing in common – they can be shattered by just one fall, by one crushing blow. These objects are great figurative comparisons to human beings, our individuality, and our sense of identity. This is because no matter how society may have labelled us, whether based on our physical, financial, educational or social state, one thing is certain – we can all come crashing down to the ground, and our lives can be shattered into a million pieces. The road to healing and restoration, however, is incumbent upon our ability to assess where we are and where it is that God is trying to take us.

I have always regarded brokenness (or feeling shattered) as the ultimate pain in life. I say this because more often than, not the force of the impact hits us on such a personal level that, for a while, our world becomes blurred and muddled. We then are compelled to ask this question: *"What makes the impact so damaging?"* Though many scholars would agree that there is no definitive answer to this question, my findings have led me to one thing - the element of surprise.

The age-old debate of surprise vs. expectation has been had on many couches and across many tables over the years, yet still no definite agreement has been made. However, in my quest to understand and interpret the effect of an impact, I've found that there are three factors that ought to be considered: **when, where** and *how.* Exactly when did this devastating event hit your life? At what point in your life were you at when this matter arose? What area of your life was targeted? What areas were affected? And, the very hardest to think about, in some cases, who was involved? Was this something that you could have avoided? Studying these factors will help you to understand, in a greater way, how Satan works and how his efforts got you here.

Bad Timing vs. Preparation

For a deeper understanding of "the *when* of an impact", the saying *"Timing is everything!"* comes to mind. Imagine dealing with financial instability when you're suddenly slapped with divorce papers from your spouse. Imagine battling a sickness, struggling to make doctor payments, and then receiving notice that the bank wants to take your home. Imagine dealing with a problem child, working an unrewarding job, and discovering that your spouse has left you for your best friend or family member. Any of these traumatic events can cause an individual to feel as if their back is against the wall, and even more so when they are facing more than one situation at a time.

It is possible that many of you reading this are in any of these situations, or you know someone who is or has been. It's not easy! When faced with such detestable circumstances, the weight of life becomes more than one can bear, and often leads to feelings of depression and hopelessness, which are telltale signs of a person who is broken or shattered.

Another factor to consider with timing is preparation. How much easier would it be to deal with life's challenges as they come if you were more prepared? But, as you know, life doesn't work that way, at least not in every case. I live in The Bahamas, and out of all the natural disasters that exists, hurricanes tend to impact us the worse. During hurricane season, or within the threat of an impending hurricane, we are charged to take the necessary precautionary measures for our home, albeit internally and externally. We seal windows, pile up sandbags to the doors, and park and secure our cars. If we are in a low-line area, we secure our grounds and evacuate to a place with little to no flooding. We stock up on non-perishable food items, first aid kits, and the list goes on. Not to mention the mandatory house insurance that provides further security. It's no secret that there is a level of peace that overcomes us when we follow these guidelines. This is because we are almost guaranteed a swift recovery. But what if we could emulate such preparatory measures for life's unexpected situations?

While some things can be prepared for, such as saving money in case of emergencies and taking care of your body to avoid certain sicknesses, we know that not every situation can be prepared for. This is one of the ineludible factors that make an impact so damaging. You see, Satan has mastered the art of ambush. He strikes when timing isn't right, and when there is little to no way to bounce back – which means his target is unassuming, vulnerable and defenseless, and after the blow, they are left graveling for the pieces of their now shattered lives. He is fully aware that TIMING is KEY!

Soft Spots

Are you familiar with the term "soft spot"? It is used to describe a physical area or topic that is sensitive to pressure. Every living thing has a soft spot, and though the human race is of the dominating species, it is of no exception. For some, financial security is a soft spot, while for others; matters of health are of greater value and importance. But I believe it is safe to say that 'relationships' – whether family or other, are the most common soft spots amongst us.

To better understand this 'soft spot' concept, think back to your childhood and try to recall a time when you were physically injured. Contemplate on the area of your body where you suffered the most pain and discomfort. Imagine having that spot struck with great force, and think about how that one strike would affect your whole body. The shock that reverberates in your body demonstrates clearly how one situation can impact our life. Once the right spot is struck in the right way and at the right time, the outcome is a pain that ripples out toward various aspects of our lives.

Our enemy, Satan, is a master predator, and attacking our 'soft spot' is a part of his modus operandi. He is very calculated and cunning, as most predators are. **In 1 Peter 5:8 (KJV) we are encouraged to,** *"Be sober, be vigilant; because your adversary the devil, as a roaring lion, walketh about, seeking whom he may devour."* We learn here that he lurks in the shadows, studies what we do and how we live daily, and waits to go after any area that is left unguarded. He is aware that our vulnerability to certain things or people will make the blow of an impact more vigorous, and it is those areas (soft spots) that he seeks to target.

Ponder for a moment on the last situation that knocked you off your feet. Were you expecting it? Did it involve a person or thing that you held near? Didn't the magnitude of the pain come as a result of the area it involved? It is natural to connect life's grievances to something you may have done wrong. But it is vital that you understand, as we transition into the "how" of an impact, that what you are experiencing now is just Satan at work, and that his game plan is simple: RIGHT TIMING plus RIGHT PLACE equals STRIKE!

Extreme Measures

TRUTH, though difficult to hear at times, is a discussion that must be had in order for the right survival plan and stance to be devised. This is why, at this juncture, I believe it is important to convey clearly that Satan's intention for your life bleeds very malicious intent. I need you to get this because, for Satan, his mission is not a game to him. Within the mind of this calculated assailant is a stream of toxic bullets that are loaded, aimed, and then fired with the sole intention to STOP YOU PERMANENTLY! See, this is no sandbox fight… this is a WAR! And to achieve success of a plan of this magnitude, Satan takes what we've coined as *"extreme measures"*. This means that his gloves are off and things are about to get messy. And that's just it, Satan plays messy!

Whenever we discuss "how" something will be done, we go into the MINUTE DETAILS, and we observe all of the intricacies of every step and procedure toward the end goal. Consider your most recent life altering situation. Think about how cunning and crafty Satan had to be to cause the blow to have the impact that it did. Let me try to bring this a bit closer to home. In most drama-filled movies that often gain mass commentary on various social media outlets, there is often an assailant…an enemy, and whether out of feelings of threat, pride, greed, or revenge, this character seeks the best way to destroy his or her target. A common thread across such movies is by reaching SOMEONE CLOSE TO THE TARGET.

I mentioned earlier that relationships are the most common soft spots that exist amongst humanity – making it one of Satan's deadliest weapons. This is where he uses tools such as deception, neglect and disdains to cause confusion and thereby inflict hurt, a hurt that spirals and ultimately destroys lives. Your loved ones become pawns in his game, and he either hurts them, or he uses them to hurt you. And this is only one way that he fights.

In the sport of boxing, players are encouraged not to make strikes below the belt. This is because the region below the belt is considered delicate or fragile territory. Rules such as this also exist in the real world. This is so that we can exist and conduct symbiotic relations and still live peaceably. Satan, however, evades these rules. He hits below the belt on purpose because he'll do ANYTHING to win. This is why "how" Satan operates is very relevant. The more you know about it, the better your chances of DEFENSE and SURVIVAL.

CHAPTER TWO
The Aftermath

What we do after an impact depicts a lot about who we are and what we are made of. In those defining moments we come face to face with where we are in God. Do we really trust Him? Can we really turn to Him? Are we really able to find peace in the scriptures that we've quoted for so many years now that it's time to apply them? Well, the aftermath is where all of these questions will be answered.

"Aftermath" is a name given to the immediate time after an unpleasant event has occurred. It's the seconds, minutes, and initial days after you got that bad news, after you've lost that job, after you've seen that report, after that budding relationship has been tarnished. The decisions you make here are vital, and be not mistaken for one moment that Satan isn't still around making jabs to see whether you are still up to fight or, as they say in wrestling, whether you have "tapped out".

Before moving on, I believe that this is a good place to tell a bit of my personal story, just in case you're thinking that you are alone in being shattered. I have had the privilege of working in the private banking industry for many years. Life was good in every way, from having financial comfort and security, to taking care of my family, to travelling the world and meeting clients. I was "living the dream" according to the world's standards, when suddenly, I had a "life shift". I guess you can say it was an epiphany moment.

I was prompted by the Holy Spirit to work for my church, a move that changed the way I viewed life entirely. I went from seeing work as a means of meeting needs and enjoying life, to an opportunity to serve others and reach more people for the glory of God. This move did a lot for my personal and spiritual development, and within less than two years, I became the leader of that church.

As can be predicted, after this change in rank, I noticed the gradual shifting of attitudes amongst some of the people in the church. Never mind that I grew up with many of them. The difference now was that I was leading them. I should also make mention here that I had become the first Black leader in the history of this local church, although it had been established for some forty-three years and held a congregation of about five hundred people. I was excited about the possibilities of where we could go. However, after a few years into this journey, the excitement came to a crashing halt in what I term as *"my fall from grace"*.

May I say that life can crash from one bad decision, one wrong turn, from meeting one wrong person, or saying one wrong word? I have to emphasize this because sometimes Satan's strategy involves planting traps, and those traps are disguised in conversations, connections and decisions that come our way. With one wrong move he'll have you exactly where he wants you, and for the broken that are reading, you can validate this. I hope you get the picture: **JUST ONE!**

Needless to say, many of the people turned on me in what seemed like an instant (my words). Remember that these were people with whom I grew up and have helped in many ways, whether financially or otherwise. At what would have been one of the roughest patches of my life, these people had spoken some of the most spiteful and vicious words against me, and even to me. I recall the atmosphere being so tense and toxic that if you lit the proverbial match, the fumes alone would cause an explosion.

For many this would have been the breaking point - suffering the public's disdain against me. But to be honest, I didn't mind this part too much because, as a former marine, I was trained to take on harsh words. In my mind, I reconciled with myself and with God; I could take what was going on. I was tough. I could handle it. Satan, in his distinctive nature, was not too far behind. In fact, he was ahead of me. He shifted his focus and set aim toward my "soft spot" – my family. When the attack turned on them, and I saw the pain that my actions had caused, the shattering felt almost instant.

The Smoke Clears

When news of what happened came to light, I felt a surfeit of emotions – anger, embarrassment, regret, fear, and confusion being amongst them. I remember mentally retracing the steps I took that led me to that place, and I wondered whether I had missed some obvious signs. This is a common train of thought for some who encounter one of Satan's deadliest strikes. We question and we blame, when admittedly (in some cases), we just couldn't see.

Mankind has always been quick emotional responders. The fallacy that has been shared around from group to group, and from generation to generation, is that women are more of the emotional reactors. On the contrary, men are emotional reactors as well. While females appear to be the most sensitive of the species, males also exhibit outbursts of emotional frustrations. Temper tantrums, being short of patience and void of any ability to understand simple logic (after an ordeal), are characteristics of a male's emotional response.

Consequently, history has proven that reacting out of emotional instability can only heighten the level of damage you will experience in any given circumstance. This advice may be too late for some of you, but I'm assured by the Holy Spirit that some of you reading are freshly broken, and you want to say and do some things that have not been sanctioned by God. Making rash decisions and spewing out words in the peak of your condition is not wise. Within the first days let the dust settle – BE STILL and HOLD YOUR PEACE.

As the days went on things got chaotic very quickly. I spent a lot of time being inconspicuous about what happened until I became like a walking dead man, and I lived like this day by day. But deep down I knew that things had to change and I had to see things turn for the better yet again. I couldn't stay where I was. I remember thinking to myself, *"How do I move from where I am?"* See, after a while, I had made up my mind that this broken state wasn't for me.

I must admit, though, that there were moments where I felt lost to life and even wondered what the use was in continuing on. However, I quickly surmised that self-pity. I knew that feeling sorry for myself and my situation was not going to make me whole, especially when I had a hand in my own breaking, which brings me to my next point.

Staying in a place that is mentally, emotionally, and spiritually toxic for you will only hinder your progress. The place that I had found myself in was harmful, but by God's grace alone, I made it out. Therefore, you must make considerable efforts to get up from this place of anger, self-pity, self-blame, regret, self-conviction, and condemnation. Get out while you can. How do you do this? By clinging to every word of hope given to you by God, and also by remembering this one word – SEASONS! Tattoo this to the front of your mind - your present state is not permanent. Once you keep this in the front of you, then you can begin to make confident strides toward wholeness.

Where was God?

Despite where you are in your brokenness, I know that many of you reading have a relationship with God. At the time of my brokenness, so did I. I thought that our relationship was exactly where it should have been, but to be transparent, I was angry with Him. I wondered why He didn't cut me some slack and ease the pain. I wondered why He didn't prevent this all from happening.

For some of you, this is where you are currently. You're in a place of resentment and utter bitterness. I can understand your thoughts, but I have to interject here by saying being angry with God won't change anything; it won't help. In fact, it will only prolong your suffering by building a levee between you and the One who can help you. What I have discovered, as I look back, is that the journey back to wholeness is life-changing and can be very rewarding. You may not be able to internalize this at the moment, but God's purpose is being fulfilled in your life. This process has a promise at the end of it, and that is to bring you out stronger, wiser, and better than ever before.

God did not promise us a bed of roses. This is something that I had to recognize. Stewing in my anger toward God and casting blame on Him only caused me to see that I was just as human as everyone else was. No title or position could protect me from being taught, tried, and tested. This is an infallible truth you too must accept. Find the understanding that helps you to see beyond what you are facing now; one that reveals who you will be in the future (God's future).

The level of your circumstance only emits how much strength has already been embedded into your makeup, and what God has predestined you to become. The saying that God only gives His toughest battles to His toughest fighters is TRUE! Ask Job! So, it doesn't matter if you are a political leader of a country who is facing lack of faith from those around you. It doesn't matter if you are the CEO of a company who was ousted by your colleagues. It doesn't matter if you have helped people and they have turned on you. Your place in life doesn't negate that you are still God's heir; one that He affirms and seeks to prove is DESTINED FOR GREATNESS. So, shake off the anger and let go of the resentment. During this "aftermath period," settle yourself quickly, and instead of turning away from God, run to Him.

James 1:2-4 (ESV) says, *"Count it all joy, my brothers, when you meet trials of various kinds, for you know that the testing of your faith produces steadfastness. And let steadfastness have its FULL EFFECT that you may be PERFECT and COMPLETE, LACKING IN NOTHING."* What does this mean for you? It's simple - God hasn't left you. He's got a plan that far exceeds what your human mind can fathom. Overcoming the sporadic turns of this life has taught me that you don't have to know, understand, or agree with what God does. What is paramount is that you know, understand, and agree with the fact that through Him ALONE, you will achieve victory.

Part Two
BROKEN FRAGMENTS

CHAPTER THREE
Facing Truth

In facing our individuality, one of the biggest challenges is recognizing that we are shattered. In some cases, it is far easier to run from discovering the truth of who we are and where we are. What is truth? Truth is that which is genuine and real. Truth is that which is reliable and authentic. Truth is God Himself; He is the standard by which everything is measured.

You see, life has a strange way of revealing things to us, and one thing that life has come to reveal to me is that one of the most difficult people in the world to deal with is one's self. Many times, we find ourselves hiding behind various masks, and we often use other vices to try to soothe our spirits and our minds. But after we have tried all of the vices, and after we have removed all of the masks, we come to discover that we are in a far worse place than before.

I have seen movies and commercials where people are at meetings, such as AA (Alcoholics Anonymous). It is interesting to note that they begin their introductions to the group by stating their names and then declaring this statement, "I am an alcoholic." In other words, they own their situation. They come to the realization that they are at a place where they need help before alcoholism kills them. These people are broken and they are in need of help. That's what these groups offer. It takes great courage and strength to admit our brokenness, but it is necessary! Once you give something an identity, you are first acknowledging that it is there, and it has a nature. From here you can learn how to deal with it.

False Facades

Today, humanity runs away from discovering who we are by trying to find ourselves through other means. In fact, we pay psychiatrists, phychics and psychologists billions of dollars annually just to tell us who we are, and we still cannot seem to find the answer. For some, suicide seems to be the order of the day, even amongst those who seem to have it all together. But sadly, in most cases, physical, financial, and even material stability doesn't help the empty and void feeling that people long to have filled and satisfied.

When broken, the devil warps our minds. We learn to find contentment in hiding behind titles, positions, connections, possessions, and statuses. But the more we hide, the further we are from true healing. Yes, as individuals, pride gets in the way, and we end up doing more harm than good to ourselves when we don't face the truth of where we are and who we are in the moment. I must confess that I am in the same boat sometimes. When you are the leader, the one at the front of the line, it seems as though a microscope is turned on us personally just to see what we are made of and whether we can stand the trials and tests that we can encounter. After all I am also human. I hid behind the expectations of being a Pastor. I hid behind the expectations of being a man – pretending to be strong and in control. But there was a hurricane of turmoil brewing on the inside, and I was on the brink of a shut down.

I hid behind denial, knowing that I had to face the music and reality sooner rather than later. I hid behind any and everything that would help me avoid my reality of brokenness and chaos. Hiding, by the way, does not help, but makes matters worse, because we cannot live in a world of fantasy forever. Life does not work that way.

How can humanity discover who we really are? This question has been asked, I'm sure, so many times. The answer, however, lies in knowing who has created us in the first place. We can never achieve real wholeness until we accept and acknowledge that we are hiding behind facades, which are temporary, false, and an illusion of what won't last and, at any moment, can come crashing down. Then and only then will we be able to face the person who we see in the mirror.

The Man in the Mirror

One of the hardest parts of the whole ordeal for me was the moment I sat at the bedside of my wife to relay to her what happened. To make matters worse, she didn't fuss. She simply asked me if I was done, and then she made a statement that stunned me. She said, *"I knew all along."* I'm pretty sure that not everyone's situation will be like this, but after the dust settles and things begin to become clear again, it is critical that you face the truth that's in front of you. This means that you have to stop, clear your mind, and think soberly, even while in the greatest pain. You have to be honest with those who you've hurt, and then you must face the dreaded "self-reflection".

Only afterwards will you be able to take ownership of your own actions.

I was facing a crucial time and I wondered where God was when I needed Him. I needed him to put my broken family back together again. The enemy began to place crazy thoughts in my mind, until one day God led me straight to **ME**. Through Him I mustered up the strength to push through the maze of frustrations and see the parts of me that needed adjusting. That is another reality that we must confront. If we are going to be whole, adjustments must be made to avoid situations that caused our brokenness in the first place.

Whatever we have encountered initially usually comes back around again. It may be in a different form, but it is the same spirit at work. The Bible reminds us that there is nothing new under the sun, and the devil really isn't that smart. He disguises the same old tricks in new packaging; therefore, vigilance is the key.

When in self-examination, it is imperative to locate your weaknesses and faults and do what needs to be done to correct them, and to become stronger in the traits that will guarantee you victory. You may be wondering what I learned in my brokenness? What did I see after being introspective? I learned that I was naïve in a lot of ways, and too trusting and accepting of people at face value. To many of you, such a lesson should be already learned by a Pastor. But as I mentioned before, I am human too, and title or not, I will fail and at times and so will you. However, it is not the end so stop beating up yourself.

Through God's timely revelation, I discovered that I must always guard myself through wisdom, and that I must be careful who I let into my space. He reminded me that I didn't always know best. I experienced the results of not trying the spirits that I encounter in others in order to discover what their motives were. Discernment and wisdom were what I needed to strengthen and build me.

A time of reflection in the midst of chaos calls for much maturity. Some people are actually able to do this on their own and are successful. After all no one knows us better than we know ourselves, right? We cannot lie to ourselves, nor can we deceive ourselves. It is hard to see the wrong in ourselves sometimes, especially if we battle with pride. The question is, are you able to take ownership for your wrongs? Are you able to see that you really aren't perfect, that you really don't know everything? If your answer is yes, then looking in the mirror won't be so hard. But if your answer is no, then we have quite a bit of work to do.

There are some of you reading who have a hard time admitting that you are broken. In fact, you are probably living in a world of perfection that you created on your own. You may also be in association with people who are enablers, in other words, people who tell you what you want to hear. It is time to wake up and experience truth. I hate to burst your bubble, but the truth is all of us have our imperfections, and we can only get help from a perfect God. Let Him work in you.

Things get better if you reflect in humility. You must admit and accept your faults, failures, and weaknesses. It doesn't mean you are beyond help. It just simply means that you have to lean on a God who is eager to direct you. Remember that it takes strength and courage to admit these things, to admit that you're broken, and even more strength to want to be made whole and go after it. What are you waiting for? Face yourself!

Let it Go

King David of The Bible was anointed, hand-picked, and chosen by God to be king over Israel, God's chosen nation, and even though God knew that He would mess up, He still anointed him long before. What does this have to do with you, you may ask? Well, God knew that you and I would face dilemmas. He knew that we would fall and make mistakes, but God still allowed us to be born into this world and to be alive to this very point.

Yes, David was disciplined by God for his disobedience and his sin, just as we are, but God meant for good that which Satan meant for evil in David's life. Do you think God wants bad for your life? Do you think you are going to be where you are forever? Not if God has anything to do with it!

What I like about God once He disciplines us for our disobedience is that He doesn't hold grudges! He doesn't remember our mistakes and faults and hold onto them and throw it back in our face. Satan does that, and he does it because he knows it will break us down. We lose our momentum to get back up, and we feel unworthy of the help that God readily has available for us. However, once what we did is done and we ask for forgiveness, God moves on and we must do so also.

After laying down your facades, and after having to face the truth of who you are, what you did, and where you are, you could be emotionally and physically spent. You can begin to feel unworthy, dirty, useless, defeated and so much more. But not only must you let your guilt go, you must also let go of what happened as well. Don't look back; just keep your eyes up and ahead. We cannot continue to hold on to our imperfections and mistakes. We cannot continue to live in the "shoulda, coulda, wouldas". It's done, it has passed, and it's time to accept things and move forward. I am sure that David carried guilt, like we do at times in our broken state. He experienced pain, just like we do. He felt hopeless, just like we do. But at some point, David decided to let it go and hold on to God, and I reiterate that so must you.

After my fall from grace, I made the decision in time to release every broken piece of my life to God. I knew that I could not do it by myself. You see, I could not change the experiences that I had, no matter how I tried to reason in my mind. In fact, it was not healthy for me or those connected to me to sit in a state of condemnation and self-pity. Through God's help, I opened myself up to his healing, and he did not disappoint me. It is amazing; out of all of my pain I am able to pen this book. By the end of this book, you will see for yourself.

S.O.S.

God has a listening ear and is always there to hear and help. He says in **Jeremiah 33:3, (KJV)** *"Call unto me, and I will answer thee, and shew thee great and mighty things, which thou knowest not."* This is God speaking and He gives us a promise. I know that you may be having a flashback in your mind right now of promises that have been made to you by people and how they have failed to fulfill their end of the bargain. But with God, He won't fail you.

Four things jump out at me from the scripture I just cited – **call, I will answer, shew thee,** and **thou knowest not.** Calling requires movement. It is an action word, as my English teacher back in the day would say. Whenever an S.O.S. signal is given, it can be seen from far away and lets onlookers know that someone needs help. It's a call. It's an action taken to bring awareness. Similarly, you must do something for God to respond. The scripture here says that when you do, He will answer. It can just be as simple as you sitting in your room, or your car, or at your desk at work, or wherever you find yourself reading in this moment, and saying quietly out of your mouth to the Lord, "I need Your help! I can't do this anymore! Help me!" This is a big enough S.O.S. to God, and He will answer!

God takes it even further and says He will show us great and mighty things, things that you could not even imagine. He is a revealer. He will show you how you got where you are, the role you played, who is really to blame and, most importantly, the way out. Wouldn't you want to know this? Wouldn't this be better than paying someone to tell you washed up advice?

"The broken" often turn to money, alcohol, drugs, sex, power, and people for help. But experience has taught many that they are only temporary fixes. The reality is clear, ultimate help and healing come from no other person but Jesus Christ. Do you want to stay where you are forever? Is your life at the best place it could be? How serious are you about your freedom? You must have a sense of desperation to be whole, and be willing to do whatever God requires you to do in order to make that happen. Allow Him to heal you in the way that He chooses, and rely on His judgement because He always wants the best for you. Remember that all things will work together for your good once you love God and are called according to His purpose **(Romans 8:28)**.

Wherever you are right now, talk to God and ask Him to give you the strength to begin the process one step at a time.

We are further reminded in His word, that a broken and contrite heart He will not despise **(Psalm 51:17)**. So, be vulnerable! Cry out! Be transparent with Him. Be willing to hear what He has to say to you and the instructions that He has to give. Know from now that things won't be easy, but in the end it will be worth it.

CHAPTER FOUR
A Purpose

Behind everything we face, everything we see, everywhere we go, everyone we meet, everything we are, there is a purpose. Purpose is the reason why something exists or takes place. It is brought clearer to us when we have been processed by life's experiences.

When it comes to our relationship with God, as painful as it may appear in the moment, brokenness is a part of these "teachable life experiences" that I'm talking about, and in the end God reveals to us that He must always be our focus. In His unpredictable way, He reminds us that our purpose is to worship Him with our entire being. He also allows us to experience how no matter what we face; He works things out for our good so that, ultimately, His purpose is fulfilled in us.

No one likes to go through brokenness. In fact, we automatically assume that Satan is just having too much fun with us. But the truth is so much can be behind what we are dealing with. There is so much behind your brokenness, and in this chapter we will look at some reasons as to why you are where you are. For some of you, it may be one reason, while for others, it may be more than one. But I can promise you that no matter what reason or reasons it may be, it will ALL work together for your GOOD as you submit it to God.

Servanthood

Servanthood is **service to God** and to our fellow man. It is a calling and our vocation. Servanthood is concerned with making people's lives better, and if I may confess, comes with many challenges. This is mostly because people can be difficult to please, and if we aren't able to deal with them as Christ would, we could find ourselves in wrong standing with God. This is one reason why God permits us to be broken. It is the best way to see the greatest manifestation of God and servanthood in our lives. Then and only then do we become, first and foremost, humble servants toward Him. After all, it is all about God, and we belong to Him, right? From this place of humility are we better able to display acts of servanthood towards others.

There are some of you readers who are reminiscing about painful moments you have encountered, some of which might have been as a result of your attempts to be a good person towards others (like I have). PEOPLE might be the very reason you are broken, and I'm sure right now the last thing you want to hear is that you are going through all of this in order to be better towards PEOPLE. I'm sure there were times that the pain seemed so unbearable, and many times, you've wondered whether you should quit or give in. In fact, the pain has caused you to become isolated, and you do not even want to be around people. But before you settle on those thoughts, let me tell you a story.

There was a man who had some friends. They went everywhere together. They saw him when he was down and when he was up. They ate together, cried together, and travelled through life together. He shared his vision with them and taught them many life lessons, which made them better along the way. As a matter of fact, they all reaped the rewards of His service to them. By now, I'm sure many of you have caught on that I'm talking about Jesus and His disciples. Yes, Jesus. He experienced such deep brokenness, but yet stayed true to His assignment (service). He was denied by one of these same friends, and even betrayed by another – all so that He may fulfill His ultimate service. But the story doesn't stop there. After Jesus had endured much suffering, He reaped FAR GREATER than He lost. Yes, He still serves us as our Lord and Master, but He has also been given a seat at the right hand of God, great power, and authority over the earth and heavenly realms.

Now I'm not saying that you or I are going to be exactly like Jesus, but we won't be far. There are great rewards ahead of you if you endure the brokenness and walk steadfastly in service to God. I'm sure you have many promises of God over your life waiting to be manifested. Just because the going is tough, it doesn't mean that you must quit. **James 1:2-4 (KJV) says,** *"My brethren, count it all joy when ye fall into divers temptations; Knowing this, that the trying of your faith worketh patience. But let patience have her perfect work, that ye may be perfect and entire, wanting nothing."* The brokenness will only make you more effective for God's use. Let this purpose propel you to move forward.

Life Lessons

As long as we are alive and on this earth, life should be seen as one big classroom, and while we are here we are learning many lessons along the way that ought to make us wiser and more mature. I am a big dog lover, and while viewing a clip on one of the social media platforms a quote caught my attention and I wish to share it with you. The speaker was a famous dog trainer who is known as Cesar Milan (The Dog Whisperer). Ironically, he came to America as an immigrant hardly able to speak English but made a name for himself training dogs. He stated, "UP IS WHEN YOU CELEBRATE AND DOWN IS WHEN YOU GAIN WISDOM." I am reminded that lessons learned in life, as in a classroom, always have a testing period to see what we have learned and how attentive we were to what we were being taught.

In the midst of our mistakes, acts of disobedience to God and our naiveté, we should always learn to develop a mentality that says quitting is not an option. At this moment, let me share an example with you. I like cleaning the yard, mowing the lawn, and digging in the soil because I find it refreshing, and it also suffices as moments of meditation for me. My wife constantly reminds me that when I am in the yard using any machinery, I should always keep myself protected, whether it is proper clothing, proper eye gear and the like. Isn't that just like God who reminds us in His Word (The Bible) in **Ephesians 6, that we should put on the whole armor of God so that we can fight against the tricks of Satan?** We listen at times, but there are times when we think that we are okay and we can handle the situation, until later on we find out that we cause more damage to ourselves than good.

There have been moments when I failed to heed her advice and would have stone or other debris hurling at me causing great pain in the process. There have also been times when I have seen blood flowing from my body and had to ask her to bandage me up. In spite of all that, even when she tells me to quit and sit a while, I am driven to continue because I know the goal is to finish the yard. So, I press on. What I have also discovered is that once I stop something, it seems harder to pick up where I left off, as the desire has weaned or the adrenalin has stopped flowing, and fatigue sets in even though the task is not complete. After suffering pain for not listening to my wife, I wear my protective clothing. Why? Because, I don't want to suffer the pain again. What is the moral of this story? Well, it's simple – Learn the lesson the first time so that there will be no repeats.

Brokenness is our classroom, and I urge you to learn from your mistakes while in this state. Why? When situations raise their ugly head again, and they will, you will know what to do. When a trap is set, you will know how to identify it and avoid it. Take note of your mistakes and the series of steps that led you to where you are, and the next time around – AVOID THEM! If you cannot recite what lesson you have learned, then you have not been attentive and risk going through another situation similar to the first.

What are some lessons that you may be learning? For some of you, it may be avoiding certain kinds of people and places. For some, it may be to be more accountable and better stewards over the things that you have been given. For others, it may be to change your mindsets or certain behaviors, and the list goes on. The reality is that we should not want to go back to a particular state that we have found ourselves in previously. So, we must be intentional about our walk before God, and most of all, we must choose to stick close to God, and to be more attentive and obedient when He speaks to us.

I have always surmised that victory does not come without a struggle or a fight. When we are wrecked with pain, and brokenness screams from every fiber of our being to quit, I wish to challenge you to keep going. Your drive paired with God's help will bring you to victory. Do not quit. You are a winner.

Subdued Flesh

Flesh is the greatest obstacle that we must keep under subjection because it always wants to be gratified, and sometimes, at any cost. I must say here that we operate as humans between two worlds **spirit and flesh.** The spirit realm is controlled by a supernatural force that is greater than us. I call Him God, the Creator of everything. In this world also operates the arch enemy of humanity – Satan, and he is the opposite of all that God wants for us. The flesh is the manifestation of this constant battleground, and depending on whom we listen too, God or Satan will determine our actions.

The Bible reveals to us in **Galatians 5:17-21** how the flesh operates when not submitted unto God. Here are a few characteristics that identifies when our flesh is not submitted to God: adultery, fornication, uncleanness, lasciviousness, idolatry, witchcraft, hatred, variance, emulations, wrath, strife, seditions, heresies, envyings, murders, drunkenness, and revellings. Can you imagine the brokenness that is caused when we allow our flesh to be controlled by these vices? There will be broken people, broken relationships, and broken families and communities. This produces people who have submerged themselves into states of confusion, frustration and despondency.

The fight against your flesh is not an easy one. The Bible says that we were born into sin and shaped in iniquity (**Psalm 51:5**). In other words, acting in flesh, or carnally, comes naturally to us. But the first step to overcoming your flesh is surrendering your life to God, and letting the Word of God guide your decisions. We need the Holy Spirit to help us, and He is there advising you about who to talk to, where to go, what to say, and when to move. All you have to do is follow that small inner voice. Submit your will and desires to Him. Once God is steering you, you will never fall.

Giving Birth

Any woman who has birthed a child can tell you that it is a painful experience. It requires a lot of work along with pushing and crying and sometimes a form of deliriousness because of the pain. I had the privilege of being in the room with my wife during the birth of our two children. In fact, in my mind, I can still feel the pain myself as she squeezed my hands so tightly. It was as if I was in labor too. But when birth came to fruition and we heard the screams of our healthy babies, it is amazing how quickly we had forgotten the pain that took place just moments before. I want to encourage you once again not to quit even though you may be in the pain of brokenness at this moment. **In the book of Isaiah chapter 66:9 (KJV) God says, "Shall I bring to the birth, and not cause to bring forth? saith the LORD: shall I cause to bring forth, and shut the womb? saith thy God?"** You will bring forth your wholeness and your joy if you stick with the process and allow God to give you the victory in your situation.

I wish to refer again as I believe we all know about King David and the many stories that surrounded him. He faced many hardships, some because of his own decisions, and others from opposition near and far. But out of David's brokenness and dysfunction came some of the greatest poetry recorded in the Bible in the book of Psalms. David also received a son, Solomon, who was later made the wisest man to have ever lived. David and Solomon are only some examples of what it is to birth after pain. What do you think will come out of your brokenness?

When God is finished with us, our lives become rich with experiences and stories that we can share. We can help others who may be going down similar roads as we did. We can share our story to bring healing to someone else. In fact, as you are reading these words, I am a living witness as this book is the birthing manifestation of my pain and brokenness.

Let me interject here that I am a big fan of country music. I can't help it! I went to University in the Southern United States, Tennessee. If you have ever listened to country music, you'll identify that the songs reveal life experiences. Sometimes I would say that the writers must have gotten the inspiration from a dark place because they tell some sad stories, but somehow most lead to a message of hope and growth.

Who knows what songs are in your belly that can be written because of your brokenness? Who knows what books are yet to be written because you did not quit? Who knows what poetry, what music, what artistry is within you? This brokenness helps you to view life from a different perspective? But you, nor the world, will ever know unless you push through the birthing season and hear the joy of your babies cry. I know you can do it. In fact, I am rooting for you. But better than me, God is rooting for you, and He is on your side. Scream if you have to; cry if you have to; moan if you have to, but do not stop pushing. For some of you, the time of birthing has come. PUSH! The pain will not be in vain, and God will bring you through.

God's Glory

I began this chapter talking about purpose. Ultimate purpose is what God desires for our life, after all, He made us in His image to be just like Him. But let's go back to the Bible for another example of "brokenness to success". There is a story about a man named Job; in fact, the book is named after him. The story begins by saying that he was wealthy materially and had an outstanding family. From the natural perspective, we would say that Job had it all together. However, in a moment, life changed, and Job lost everything, including all of his children. He was reduced to scraping his skin with broken pottery while he sat in the dust, as boils were over his body, and he was trying to ease the physical pain.

Every time I read his story, I am fascinated by the fact that God and Satan had a conversation about Job without his knowledge, discussing how he would be broken and stripped of everything. It just confirms that God is truly the omniscient (all knowing) one, and nothing we go through catches Him by surprise. Through the process, the pain became so unbearable that Job even cursed the day that he was born. We all have weak moments like this in our pain and say some things in the process that are crazy when we look back on it.

To top it off, he had friends who tried to console him but were not doing a great job. They accused him of sinning against God as the reason for his brokenness. To add insult to injury, his wife told him to curse God and die. This continued for a while, and it seemed as though Job even got a bit delirious as he tried to reason with God, but to no avail. For some of you, doesn't this sound familiar? I've found that sometimes God makes the situation so difficult that you aren't able to turn to friends or family for encouragement or guidance. The only thing left to do is turn to Him.

In the fullness of time, God confronted Job with a series of questions, showing His sovereignty and power, and Job had to keep his mouth shut because he did not have any answers to God's questions. He came to the conclusion that he was but frail humanity and needed God. The story concludes that Job was blessed by God with double what he had previously. Ultimately God was glorified, and His purpose was fulfilled in Job's life because Job had an even closer walk with God after his brokenness. God was able to prove to Satan that His trust in Job was merited. He never went back to losing his wealth and family again, and lived in prosperity until the day he died. God got the glory and Job lived to tell the story. There are some experiences I believe that God would not allow us to go through again. After all, God works in His own way to bring us into wholeness.

I always say that God gives His toughest tests to His strongest children. He believes in us, so all we have to do is believe in ourselves and trust Him to see us through to the end. Then, and only then, when we look back, and when the world looks at us, THEY WILL KNOW THAT IT COULD ONLY BE OUR ONE TRUE AND LIVING GOD. So, my encouragement for you in this chapter is not to live in your negative experiences. It's not going to end here...THAT IS A PROMISE! Live in God and in your present reality of hope. God is the lifegiver. He specializes in taking our life pieces that are chipped, broken, and scarred, and making a beautiful vessel out of it for His glory. You have been destined to rise from your grave of death, pain, defeat, loneliness, and despair. Satan can try, but he cannot hold you down. God will be glorified in your life. Resurrection is coming!

CHAPTER FIVE
Jagged Edges

Being broken is not only a detriment to ourselves, but also to other people. To illustrate my point, if you or I were to walk among any form of shattered pieces, there would be splinters in our feet, causing pain and making it difficult to walk. Similarly, when we are shattered spiritually, emotionally, or mentally, it affects those around us, and we can cause them pain. We can affect their confidence, their beliefs, and even their ability to move forward in life. In other words, attaining your healing is more important than you know. People are depending on it.

Close Contact

Sad to say, during these times of emotional instability and fragility, those closest to us suffer the most hurt, pain, abuse, and neglect. The saying that, *"Hurt people, hurt people,"* proves to be very true at times like these. Sometimes hurt people cause hurt intentionally, because they don't want to feel hurt alone, and sometimes the transfer of that hurt is unintentional. Nonetheless, at some point or the other, those around us and close to us will suffer a bit. The million-dollar question though, is HOW DO WE AVOID IT?

At the beginning of this chapter, I drew an illustration of a broken glass (hurt person) coming into contact with someone, and the hurt and bleeding that it can cause. There are two probable causes for this, The first being that the hurt person was careless about how they dealt with people or situations during their period of brokenness, leaving little thought to how others would be affected and The second being that those around the hurt person weren't careful in how they approached or dealt with the afflicted individual, allowing room for their own mental and emotional lacerations.

When in a "jagged" state, honesty about where you are emotionally, mentally, and spiritually will prevent many wounds and many misunderstandings. Truthful communication puts everyone in a place where conscious efforts NOT to mishandle each other are made, and for the most part, can be successful.

If we want to be whole, and see those connected to us whole, then we must do whatever it takes to stop the bleeding. My wife, I must say, has a quiet personality, but she is no push over. After my fall from grace, it was as if I watched the Jericho wall collapse from around my wife, and I watched her bleed out hurt. My son and daughter bled also, even my extended family was bleeding. I was bleeding, and I grew tired of seeing my loved ones hurt. I had accepted the part I played in things, and came face to face with the fact that I was hurting and hurting others. So, I made a decision to be helped.

In our state of brokenness, it is imperative that we associate ourselves with people who are stronger than us- to whom we can be accountable, and to whom help can be provided as we channel through life's moments of pain. The bible in **Romans 15:1** speaks to this effect when we are reminded that those who are strong ought to bear the infirmities of the weak. The goal is to be strong and whole again so that we can be with the ones that we love and stop the bleeding that was caused by them walking amongst our jagged edges.

Furthermore, while we are being healed, those around us who have been affected also need to receive their healing completely. They too need to be around stronger people who can lead them back to a place of wholeness. This is the time when we all need to experience real friends who are looking out for our best interest, and are not afraid to speak truth to us, even though it may seem painful and unfair in the moment.

As it is with walking through broken glass, we must walk tenderly and carefully. Sometimes, it may mean that we have to stop a while and be by ourselves, just us and God, until our minds are back in a safe place. Whatever we need to do, we must look beyond our present state and recognize that others who are being affected by our brokenness need to see us whole again. As a husband and father, I knew that the wholeness of my family depended on my wholeness. I was driven by the need to be the husband, father, and minister that God destined me to be.

I am reminded of being in the hospital a few years ago having to have an appendix operation. I was lying in pain rolling on the floor in the early morning hours because I did not want to wake my wife (who is a trained nurse by the way). When I could not take the pain any longer, I woke her and, after asking a few questions, she told me to get in the car. She recognized it as appendicitis and was taking me to the hospital immediately.

To cut a long story short, even though I did not like hospitals, it was there that I needed help to stop the pain. I learned later that my appendix had to be removed and I arrived in the nick of time because it ruptured just as the doctors were taking it out. What am I saying? Sometimes we have to be removed from the things that caused us to be broken, and as painful as it may be in the moment, when we are made whole we will discover that it was for our own good. There is too much at stake. We do not have time to waste, so stepping out of our comfort zone and doing what God says must be done in order to save ourselves.

Caution

The goal of being whole is not to revert to the broken state that you found yourself in previously. Wisdom tells us that we ought not to go back into situations from which we have been delivered. It means that we cannot put ourselves in compromising situations, nor can we hang around people who do not want the best for our lives. This is what exercising caution is all about. It's about a heightened sensitivity to everything and everyone around you, as well as an intentional effort to live circumspectly.

As I have stated at the very beginning of the book, you must limit the element of surprise in your life. You must ask God to show you the signs that are leading back to the road of brokenness so that you can avoid them at all costs. Exercising caution requires intentionality, focus, consistency, and discipline. It requires discernment and a higher level of vigilance in every aspect of your life. To overcome brokenness is equivalent to giving your opponent a STRIKE OUT. You might have gotten hit, but you got up and you won! So, if that means that you have to run, do it. Run as fast as you can to get as far away from that path as possible.

Exercising caution also means that you need to be honest with yourself and with those connected to you. Admit your weaknesses and ask for help from those who CAN help. Ultimate help comes from God, our Creator, and we must always keep an open ear to hear what He is saying to us, so that we may learn and obey. After all, He knows what is best for us. While having God to help is FIRST, there must also be someone in the physical world that you can rely on. This is where ACCOUNTABILITY comes in.

We all need someone to talk to, and someone who we can trust to share our frailties with. Someone who won't look at us differently but would do whatever it takes to keep us whole. I'm certain that you are thinking that finding such an individual is not possible in today's world, but if you ask God to show you that person, or to send you that person, He will. The scripture where God says that man was not meant to be alone doesn't only apply to the area of marriage, but I believe overall relationships in general. There is a "help meet" out there for you when coming out of this valley of brokenness; you just have to be open to His suggestions.

This is a good place right here to talk about wholeness through the agency that God works through in the earth, and that is the church. I know for some of you, you may not think this is so because your brokenness and greatest pain came from the church, those who profess to have a relationship with God and should be a help rather than a hindrance. But the reality is that the church is made up of humanity just like us, with faults and failures. But, unlike the world, we are daily striving to be like God.

In spite of it all, it is imperative that the church be a place of healing and refuge. It must also be a group of people who are mature, patient, and always want to exhibit the heart of Jesus Christ, the One in whom we follow. Something like this goes both ways, though. Not only must the church not condemn or cast broken people aside, but so must those who have been hurt or negatively affected by the church. Now, before you discard this book, I want you to hear me out.

I mentioned earlier that the church is you and me, that is, regular people who battle with inconsistencies and imperfections daily. And while the magnitude of the hurt that we feel is deep because it is THE CHURCH, we mustn't rule out the purpose or effectiveness of the church as a whole because of the failure of man. To do that would be to tell God that He doesn't know what He is doing, and that what He has created is a failure.

Why am I saying this? In a period of caution, no one should be running away from the church. That is what Satan wants, to lead lambs astray from the security found in their flock and under their shepherd. It's only those who are mature and those who can see and understand the plots of Satan who will find themselves still believing in what God has destined His church to be – a safe haven, a place for refueling and regenerating. But does that mean that the church is always right? Does that mean that we should continue to throw water under the bridge and allow negative things to stay as is? The answer is NO.

The true church that Jesus Himself is building is a people of love, grace, forgiveness, understanding, patience, and all that is good. We shouldn't go to church because of the people, but because of the God of the people. We shouldn't forgive and love because of people, but because of the God that we serve.

So, as you exercise caution, be open for the way in which God will bring your healing. It could be through one or two people, or it could be through a church. You never know what avenue He will use. If you are smart, you won't allow the brokenness you are facing to cause you to linger in hurt and resentment. Wallowing in this place of bitterness and sorrow for too long will affect everyone and everything.

What's the bottom line? In order for you to be safe to be around again, you must get up from where you are, accept the hand of help extended toward you, and go after the life that you were destined to live. Let me submit to you that you are a champion, no matter how shattered your life may be right now. Defeat is only permanent if you stay there! Rise up, open your eyes, and trust the Spirit of God as He leads.

Part Three
THE ASSEMBLING

CHAPTER SIX

Fragility

On most occasions, after being hurt or going through a life-changing experience that has wounded us, we aren't the best people to be around. Not only are we temperamental, but we are unstable, undependable and, most of all, vulnerable. We face the dilemma of either over thinking what will happen in our lives next, or we don't think about it enough. Either way, it is relatively clear that the choices we make from this point will determine how quickly we bounce back and what will become of us after the episode of brokenness has ended. This presents a need for us to hear clear, sensible voices and be amongst people who will speak truth to us in compassion, tenderness, and genuine love for our well-being. Thus, who we allow in our lives is vital. Who and what we listen to, and even where we go, are all crucial to our successful transition from the chaos of brokenness to the peace and comfort of being whole and complete.

I must warn you as you ponder on your life and those in it, that your biggest enemy (Satan) doesn't just give in because you desire change and healing. He will continue to fight against you, just differently. When you are broken and vulnerable, there are many who come out of the wood works claiming to want to help you. They all have advice, and they all want to be there for you, but not all of them can be trusted. Not all of them are from God. In this chapter, I will shed light on some of these characters in hopes that you will be more vigilant in your dealings during your most fragile state.

1. The Jailer

I characterize the jailer as a person who enjoys seeing you broken and defeated. These individuals don't want more for your life. In fact, in some twisted sense of reality, they secretly think you deserve to be in the state that you are in. They smile with you but converse slanderously about you behind your back. They find joy in your pain and want to be the crutch in your life that you run back to every time. Let's think about it! If a prisoner is in need of anything while confined to a cell, who do they have to call on? A jailer, and if you know anything about jailers, they have very little compassion for prisoners. They want to see them bound and locked up so that justice can be served.

A jailer can be easily identified if you're looking with the right eyes. As with most "friends" or "counsellors", jailers come in a guise to help, but have their own secret agendas. Whether to build up their fragile self-image or to seek revenge, jailers stay around to make sure you don't get up again. They give you incomplete advice, causing you to be greatly dependent upon them. They even encourage pity parties. They would rather you accept the way things have panned out for your life and offer little to no words of hope. It is possible to confuse friends who "keep it real" with "jailers", but one way to tell them apart is by their words. Keep an ear out for the advice that follows them "being real." Is what they are saying really constructive for you?

2. The Dictator

This particular individual is one of the easiest to identify because of their strong personality. Dictators like the game "Simon Says". Brokenness doesn't hinder their desire to be in control. Dictators come along for the "dreary" ride only to force their views and opinions on you and tell you what to do. They believe that only what they say can help you and that outside of them, you won't make it. You see, their overall agenda is to prove to you and to others that you're still incapable of leading a successful life without them. You should know that individuals such as this see you as weak, double-minded and unstable, and this view of you is held even outside of brokenness. In other words, whether you are facing hard times or not, a dictator sees you as "the bottom, below, and insignificant."

There are many who say that they wouldn't allow someone to dictate their paths, but it is important for you to consider that when you are in a fragile state, your initial sense of awareness is weak. Your walls of defense are down, which means that influence from an outside force will be much easier. You may be wondering how you can avoid being controlled. This is simple. Do what YOU BELIEVE IS NECESSARY FOR YOU. It's all about what you feel in your heart and spirit is the right thing to do. All living things are driven by emotions, but in a case of fragility, emotions cannot be your thermostat. Set a goal for where you want to be, and with God's help, the steps will be laid out. Take the steps that you deem needed to recover. Your no means NO; your yes means YES, and by no means should you compromise your future to build a dictator's ego.

3. The Manipulator

Manipulators are some of the hardest people to detect if you are not vigilant or discerning. A manipulator's end game is themselves. Everything they say and do is to help them to get what they want. Manipulators are the people who come along and try to make you into what they want you to be. These people are related to the dictator except they have their own plans for you.

Manipulators strike during your moment of weakness and use this as a point of entry to mess up your life. That is when you are most pliable and moldable. That is when you are most accessible. It may seem like a lot to watch when you are trying to get yourself together, but a word to the wise - be watchful of who is circling your life or has entered your life during the rough patches. Some are God-sent, while others are hell-bent.

4. The Helpmate

While on the topic of those who come in and out of your life during brokenness, it would be remiss of me not to point out the group of people who God has deemed as your "helpmates". **In Genesis 2:18 God said it is not good that man should be alone, but instead that a helpmate be made for him.** Throughout teachings and preaching, many have limited this text to just marital relevance, but I wish to shed light that this also includes partnerships and relationships in its entirety.

The helpmate is the person who God has sent and designed to help you out of the broken place that you are in. These are the people who have been graced with the spiritual strength, knowledge, and patience to guide you back to wholeness. Sometimes God sends one, but in some cases, it can be more than one.

Helpmates are true to their names. They help! They see beyond where you are and into the future that God has for you. These people won't allow you to stay where you are, and they know that God has a plan for you. These individuals will guide you into God's instructions and God's ways even if you are kicking or screaming. It is vital to identify your helpmate or helpmates. The sooner you do, the sooner you can detach from anyone reflecting the image of the jailer, dictator, and manipulator.

I have discovered that the key to it all is to have a heightened sense of discernment in order to tell who is for you and who is trying to destroy you. Because God is on our side and He wants the best for us, we simply have to ask Him to show us the way, and He will do just that. In fact, He will guide and lead us through the maze of confusion and bring us to a position of clarity and wisdom. Try it, if you have never done so before. Ask Him now; you will be amazed by His response because He will never let you down.

CHAPTER SEVEN
Piece by Piece

The challenge to our individuality is not only to recognize that we are shattered, but also to know when we need help, and to whom do we turn to ask for this help. Shattered pieces can never pick themselves up. There has to be someone or something that is whole who can help along the way. To live by the foolish ideology that you can function and do this on your own is exactly that – FOOLISH!

Take for an example a car that crashes. It cannot take itself to the garage. It needs a wrecker (some of you say a tow truck) to pick it up and carry it from the accident scene. In the same manner, a sick person cannot heal themselves. They need the assistance of a doctor who has the antidote for their sickness.

With this being the case, a depraved humanity needs a perfect and holy God to make us clean and whole. We are like dirty and soiled laundry, needing tide to make us clean again. We need the hand of God to rebuild us again.

I know that in spite of all that you have already read, there are some of you who may still think that life is hopeless and that your situation is hopeless. But you are the right candidate for whom God works on. Those situations that seem impossibly hopeless are the very ones in which God is at His best.

But you have a part to play here. You must push your limit to trust Him and believe that He can fix you. The mere fact that you are alive means that there is still hope. Come on, have a spirit of expectancy that things will get better, and then watch as they do. What do you have to lose?

The Potter

No matter how we may try to deny it, there is someone greater than us and His name is God Jehovah. He is the creator of all things and all people. Nothing exists outside of God. There are so many false gods that are deceiving the minds of humankind and yet these gods cannot speak, see, hear, or reason enough to tell us who we are.

There are some of you reading this book who does not believe in this God in whom I believe. You don't believe that He can help you out of this dilemma, but I wish to challenge you to talk to Him right now. Give Him a try! I guarantee that it will be the best decision on your road to success and victory in this life. You may not believe in Him, but it won't take anything from you to talk to Him. You'll be surprised to hear what He has to say about your situation and how He can help.

To acquire an understanding of who God is, ultimately builds our understanding of who we are. Just as we spend time (in the natural) with our parents to discover who we are in our natural families, the same must be done with God. Spend time with God to discover who you are in Him. You must develop a relationship with Him, a sense of intimacy that keeps you close to Him. Once you discover who He is, then you'll find yourself, and in finding yourself, you can become content with who you are, and healing would have taken its course.

A very interesting story is recorded in the Bible in **Jeremiah 18**. The prophet is sent by God to view the workings at the potter's house. I could only imagine the scenery in the house. I guess it might look like a carpentry shop with pieces of wood scattered everywhere over the floor or just placed on a shelf in a jumbled state until the carpenter had a vision of what he wanted them to become. On the other hand, I guess it also looked like the emergency room of a hospital with broken bodies waiting to be served. When we read the story, it is interesting to note that even though the vessel being molded by the potter was chipped and cracked in places, the potter did not give up in fashioning this vessel into one of beauty.

In the final analysis, it does not matter how chipped and scarred the pieces of your life are because of all that you have encountered. God has made you a winner, and if you would allow Him, He would mold your life into something wonderful and whole. When He spins you on His potter's wheel, He will smooth you out better than anyone can.

To know God is to trust Him. As He puts the pieces of your life together and begins to add and take away from your life, He will give you strength and understanding. Whether your actions led to your broken state or not, in His assembling of you, the Master Potter will build you with so much strength and boldness that you will be able to stand, knowing that He will keep and protect you, not only through this process, but through any of life's changing seasons. You will feel comfortable with your strengths and weaknesses because you'll understand that God is with you every step of the way to guide and lead you in the right direction.

As the Potter, God pays close attention to you. In **Psalm 17:8** we are described as the apple of God's eye. This illustration indicates that just as the pupil is the center of our natural eye that funnels vision and focus, during this time of mending, God's vision and focus is centered on you. He has set apart choice people who will come in and out of your life to further teach you, guide you, and lead you to a place of restoration. We've learned about them in our previous chapter. If your reliance is fully on God to heal you, then the traffic of people in and out of your life will be smooth.

YOU – The Clay

In order to be healed by God, we ought to be moldable. We cannot fight against what God wants to do. My mind goes back to the moments when I was a child. During class time the teacher would give each child a lump of clay to make whatever we desired until playtime was complete. Led by our individual imaginations, our hands would mold that lump into what we were processing in our minds. For some of, us it was elaborate. We could make what looked like humans with all of the intricate parts. For some, we would just roll the clay into a ball and throw it up in the air until we were bored. For some, we would make animal figures and make believe that we were farmers and so much more.

What was so interesting was the number of times each one of us would smash our clay back to a lump and start all over again as our young imaginations wandered. The clay did not fight against the molding from our small hands, nor did it complain about being pinched and shaped. The clay allowed us to use it for whatever our imagination said.

Let us pivot for a moment and compare this illustration to God, our Creator, and us as His Creation. God is the potter, and we, his creation, are the clay. God has a plan for our lives, and He knows what He is doing as He molds us to comply with His plan, which is for our best interest. Sometimes it may appear painful, and, in our humanity, we may find ourselves fighting against God or as the phrase has been coined, "kicking against the prick." The reality is that because God has given us freedom of choice, He allows us to do what our heart desires. Usually this leads to devastation, brokenness, and the worst kind of pain. This is pain that could have been avoided if we would just have submitted ourselves to God's leading. The sad reality is that when we are left to our own devices, some never survive their state of brokenness because it ultimately leads to death and destruction, instead of life and wholeness.

At times, for some of us, we lament that God does not want us to have fun to enjoy life as we please. The truth of the matter is that God is saving us from pain that He knows we will encounter with our choices because He sees and knows all things. I assure you that when God is through with us, we will come out better than we could even imagine. That is a promise that He has made to us, and His promises are true and can be relied upon to come to pass. The bible puts it like this in **Jeremiah 29:11 (KJV),** *For I know the thoughts that I think toward you, saith the Lord, thoughts of peace, and not of evil, to give you an expected end."*

The Blueprint

When we are still in the presence of God, we discover our uniqueness. We become solidified in who we are, and therefore, cannot be swayed by the culture of the day, because cultures, as we know it, are always changing. We won't be defined or swayed by who others say we are because our identity would be known. But what does God say about our identity?

In the Bible, God's word and blueprint for successful living, He outlines the way we ought to be. Let's take a look at **Genesis 1:26-27(KJV)**. It states, *"And God said, Let us make man in our image, after our likeness: and let them have dominion over the fish of the sea, and over the fowl of the air, and over the cattle, and over all the earth, and over every creeping thing that creepeth upon the earth. So God created man in His own image, in the image of God created He him; male and female created He them."* The creator of everything made you and me in His image and His likeness and gave us the ultimate job description – to have dominion and rule over that which He has created. He wants us to manage it on His behalf. This is our foundation!

In **2 Timothy 1:7 (KJV)** it states, *"For God hath not given us the spirit of fear; but of power, and of love, and of a sound mind."* You learn here that any other such way of behaving and thinking is unlike God's original makeup of you and me. So, what do we do? We walk in power, we live in love, and we operate with a sound mind. Do not allow fear to prevent you from regaining control of your life. What landed you here the first time won't work another time, UNLESS YOU LET IT. You are full of power! Jesus himself said that He gave us power to tread upon scorpions and serpents. He gave you the power even over ALL the powers of the enemy **(Luke 10:19)**. These are only some of the scriptures that define your blueprint. His Word (The Bible) is there to define you and to guide you. If you read it, take it in, and apply it to your daily life, there isn't anything that you cannot face and overcome. Go back to the BLUEPRINT-God's word. Believe it and live by it!

Expanding in knowledge of the power of God's word ought to cause you to hold your head high. It should also strengthen your trust in the hands of God to mold you and put you back together again. Inside of you is the DNA of God. His very breath is in you. From the foundation of the earth God knew you, and He knew who you were destined to become. Trust Him to make you into who He has called you to be and let Him put the pieces of your life, of your heart, and of your mind back together again.

CHAPTER EIGHT
Wholeness

The Apostle Paul tells us in **2 Corinthians 5:17 (KJV)** "**Therefore if any man be** in Christ, **he is** a new creature: old things are passed away; [and] behold, **all things are become new.**" Having risen out of the ashes of brokenness, you are now a NEW CREATION in God. What you have just endured, the lessons you would have learned, are going to be put to the test. You are no longer at a crossroad but are on a clear path, and are also better positioned to make your own decisions, face challenges, overcome your own failures, and enjoy the sweet taste of success. Having survived the shattered moments and allowing God to put you back together, you are not who you were before. This time you are stronger; you are wiser; you are BETTER!

The Road Ahead

I've always been fond of what the Apostle Paul said to the **Philippians in chapter 3 verse 13 (NIV) –** *"Brothers and sisters, I do not consider myself yet to have taken hold of it. But one thing I do: Forgetting what is behind and straining toward what is ahead,"* Here he shares with them that in order to collide with God's destiny for your life, you must be adamant about pressing forward and leaving the past in the past.

Being at a place of wholeness in God presents you with an obligation of forward progression, which further compels you to become more focused than you have ever been before. It's a time when you need to remind yourself of the positive messages that have been declared over your life. It's a time to get back on the track that you were destined to trot upon.

Releasing the past is easier said than done, but it is necessary. You can never get where you are going if you are always looking back. You cannot embrace your new opportunities and relationships if you keep comparing them with the old. A truly whole person is able to FORGIVE and LET GO! That means forgiving those who have hurt or offended you and surrendering to God's will for your life.

Taking old feelings and old mindsets into a new place can cause repeat offenses, and sooner or later, you will end up right back where you were before. Looking forward and pressing forward, letting go and moving on will show God that you are trusting where He has to take you next. And while it may be hard to leave the past in the past, do it. Take only the lessons that you have learned and the strength that you have gained.

The Thought and Sight Connection

As you make preparation to launch out into the world, I wish to remind you that what you think and what you see are directly related. What you see can affect how you think, and what you think can affect how you see. **Proverbs 23:7 says that**

as a man thinks, so is he. (KJV) This is where the mindset of faith and the language of faith steps in.

Faith affects how you think and how you see. It is the wind that you need beneath your wings as you soar through the ups and downs of humanity. After being broken, you can find yourself afraid to move forward, afraid to step out and take chances. You can find yourself afraid to open up to others, afraid to try new things or go new places. But if you view life through the eyes of faith, then the way you live, the way you handle situations and tests, will yield better results.

Your Words

Having looked at the effects of your thoughts and your sight to your move forward, I want to touch the power of your words. The Bible reveals to us in **Proverbs 18:21 (KJV)** that *"Death and life are in the power of the tongue: and they that love it shall eat the fruit thereof."* What does this mean for your move forward? Simply stated – if you speak life over yourself, over your family, marriage, ministry, or business, then you will see the good fruit that life would bring. If you decide to speak death and doom and gloom, then you will see the bad fruit that death brings. It is important that your speech doesn't betray where God has positioned you.

Your words have the power to shape your future. While you can be certain that you will face hard times again, what you speak over you and your circumstances can set the atmosphere for victory or defeat. You must declare the outcome you want and believe that the God about whom you speak has the ability and the capacity to cause your words to come to pass. Allow this to register in your spirits and declare it over your life. Declare that you live a life of wholeness and completeness in every area of your life.

As we have arrived at the end of this journey, remember that what manifests as problems for us in the natural are first carried out in the spiritual realm. We often end up in broken situations when we try to deal with spiritual issues in a natural way. Spiritual battles can never be fought by human knowledge and human power, and that is why it is so important to know God and consult Him at all times when battles are raging. To think that you can handle any such matters naturally would be unwise.

Do not become over-confident or over-zealous but be careful about everything. While life indicates that there is vitality and vigor, joy and laughter, you will have uproars. When you do, you can access the peace God has for you and allow Him to lead your actions, and work on your behalf. In all things remember to - *"Trust in the Lord with all thine heart; and lean not unto thine own understanding. In all thy ways acknowledge him, and he shall direct thy paths."* **(Prov. 3:5-6, KJV)**

CONCLUSION
To The Winners

You've made it! You are here...complete and whole. You've faced yourself and you've faced defeat. You've overcome the hard times and the dark times, and now you have a testimony. You've graduated from soldier to warrior and can live to tell the story. This is what life with God is all about – overcoming obstacles by His grace.

We have encountered a lot throughout this book, but I thought it would be good to leave some tips that you can come back to if you need a reminder.

Despite how you may feel, you are equipped!

God has given you the strength and the capacity to survive any storm that comes your way. He is with you throughout the storms of life and will lead you into the path that you ought to take. With Him on your side, you will emerge from every experience with a testimony that will encourage others when on their journey.

Tests and trials are inevitable.

Do not get comfortable. Stay on alert because life is not perfect. Tests and trials will come no matter what. This is because they produce patience and strength, and they build your faith in our unseen God. From a biblical perspective, you will discover that every person who was used mightily by God encountered some level of brokenness. The popular story of Joseph is a great example. He was literally thrown into a pit alone. He encountered so much fight. Satan was having a field day with His life, but because He remained yielded to God, there was a way out. Whether you face brokenness or not, God has an entirely different script than Satan, one that names you the victor.

Go to God for help!

You cannot make it through this life without God. You cannot face the extremities of this life without Him. He is everything for you, from defense and provider, to healer and peace giver. Even if you fall and encounter brokenness once again as a result of your own doings, run to God for help. A lot of broken people existed in the Bible, but the common thread amongst them was that they knew to come to God. They recognized that He was the only one who could help and heal them all at the same time.

You are victorious!

1 John 4:4 (KJV) says, *"Ye are of God, little children, and have overcome them: because greater is He (God) that is in you,*

than he (Satan) that is in the world." What does this guarantee? Victory! You can rest assured that because you are more than a conqueror, no matter the battle you have to fight, you are not alone. God is fighting on your behalf, and you're going to come out the winner!

The Charge

I declare into your destiny that God's favor is upon you as you submit it all to Him. Whatever situation you may be in today, I call you out of your brokenness and into wholeness. Grab a hold of your future! Let the healing waters now flow upon you, your life, your family, and relationships. God has given you the fortitude to survive. Just grab a hold of it and believe. Rise up man of God; rise up woman of God and experience the abundant life that God has already prepared for you!

REMEMBER ALWAYS THAT YOU HAVE BEEN BROKEN TO WIN!

About the Author

Bishop Lester M. Cox is the Senior Pastor of *Word of Truth Ministries International*, a Non-Denominational Church situated in Nassau, Bahamas. He, along with his wife, Elder Vanessa Cox, founded this Ministry in 2007 after leaving a denominational Ministry , and through God's divine guidance, continues to experience growth and success.

He has been privileged to have preached in the United States, India, Bermuda, The Caribbean, and Latin America and has broadcasted his messages on The Word Network, U.S.A, MTM TV, Jamaica and ZNS Television, Cable 12 and ILTV in Nassau, Bahamas.

Bishop Cox is a tenacious man of great vision who desires to see the broken made whole through the power of Jesus Christ. He also enjoys spending time with his beautiful wife, and their two kids Lester Matthew and Hilary Amanda.

www.ingramcontent.com/pod-product-compliance
Ingram Content Group UK Ltd.
Pitfield, Milton Keynes, MK11 3LW, UK
UKHW022216230426
12048UKWH00016BA/872